Questions AND Answers

PLANET EARTH

Sarah Reed

KINGFISHER
NEW YORK

KINGFISHER
LONDON & NEW YORK

Published in the United States by Kingfisher, 175 Fifth Avenue, New York, NY 10010
Kingfisher is an imprint of Macmillan Children's Books, London.
All rights reserved.

Distributed in the U.S. by Macmillan, 175 Fifth Avenue, New York, NY 10010
Distributed in Canada by H.B. Fenn and Company Ltd., 34 Nixon Road,
Bolton, Ontario L7E 1W2

Library of Congress Cataloging-in-Publication Data
Reed, Sarah (Sarah M. M.)
    Questions and answers: planet Earth / by Sarah Reed.—1st ed.
        p. cm.
    Includes index.
        1. Earth—Miscellanea—Juvenile literature. [1. Earth—Miscellanea.
    2. Questions and answers.] I. Title.

    QB631.4 .R44 2001
    550—dc21   2001029004

ISBN 978-0-7534-5372-8

Kingfisher books are available for special promotions and premiums.
For details contact: Special Markets Department,
Macmillan, 175 Fifth Avenue, New York, NY 10010

For more information, please visit www.kingfisherpublications.com

Printed in China

10 9 8 7 6 5 4 3

3TR/0209/TIMS/UNV/128MA

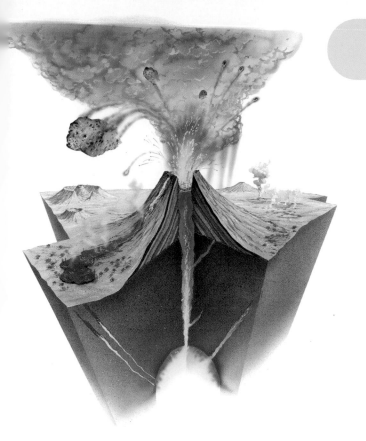

Contents

Earth's Formation

In the vastness of outer space lies a star system, or galaxy, known as the Milky Way. Inside this galaxy is our solar system—a bright star orbited by eight planets. The planet that is third closest to this star, which we call the sun, is a unique, life-supporting planet called Earth.

How did Earth form?

1 The sun was formed when a nebula—a vast cloud of gas and dust—shrank under the pull of gravity. Hot clouds of dust and gases spun around the newly formed sun.

2 When specks of this dust collided, lumps formed. Gravity pulled these lumps together, creating a large, spinning, fiery ball. Heavy elements like iron sank to the center of the molten ball.

3 Lighter metals and rocks rose to the surface of the ball, which cooled enough for a solid, hard shell to form.

Why is Earth unique?

Earth is a rocky planet that is more than one million times smaller than the sun. Unlike the other seven planets in the solar system, Earth has water and an atmosphere that contains oxygen. This means that life can exist on Earth.

4 Gases escaped from the planet and formed an atmosphere with clouds. As rain fell oceans were formed, which contained oxygen-producing plants.

5 Over time the planet became the one we live on today—but planet Earth continues to change.

Who proved that Earth is round?

For thousands of years it was a common belief that Earth was flat. After all, it appears flat to the naked eye. But in 1522 Spanish explorer Ferdinand Magellan's ship *Victoria* completed a historic journey—it sailed all the way around the world. This proved once and for all that Earth was round.

Who was Copernicus?

Before 1500 most people believed that the sun and the planets revolved around Earth. In 1530 Polish astronomer Nicolaus Copernicus (left) wrote a book showing that Earth spins on an axis and, along with the other planets, journeys around the sun. His ideas outraged many people, and the book was banned until 1830.

Copernicus

How long does Earth take to orbit the sun?

It takes 365.25 days (one year) for Earth to complete its orbit around the sun. At the same time, Earth spins on an axis that runs from the North Pole to the South Pole. It takes 24 hours (one day) for Earth to spin all the way around once on its axis.

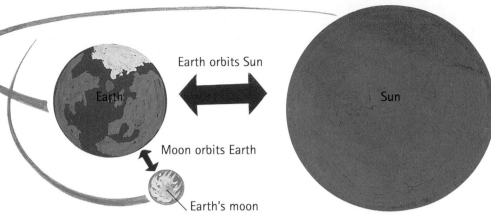

Earth orbits Sun

Earth

Sun

Moon orbits Earth

Earth's moon

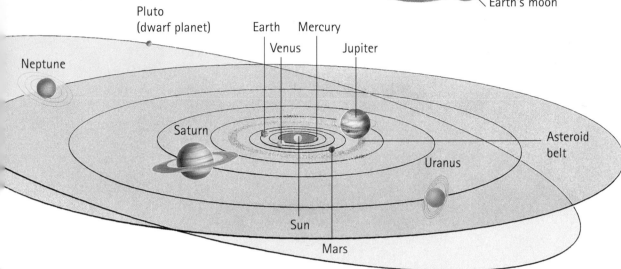

Pluto (dwarf planet)
Earth   Mercury
Venus   Jupiter
Neptune
Saturn
Asteroid belt
Uranus
Sun
Mars

Is Earth the only rocky planet?

No. The eight planets of our solar system are divided into two groups—rocky planets and gaseous or icy planets. The four planets closest to the sun—Mercury, Venus, Earth, and Mars—are rocky. Jupiter, Saturn, Uranus, and Neptune are gaseous or icy planets.

How old is Earth?

Earth formed at the same time as the sun and the other seven planets of our solar system. By studying rocks and fossils, scientists have estimated that this was around 4.6 billion years ago.

Quick-fire Quiz

1. What is a nebula?
a) A cloud of gas and dust
b) A shooting star
c) A big bang

2. How many planets are there in our solar system?
a) Five
b) Seven
c) Eight

3. When did Copernicus write his famous book ?
a) 1430
b) 1530
c) 1630

4. How long does it take Earth to spin once on its axis?
a) 24 hours
b) 30 days
c) 365.25 days

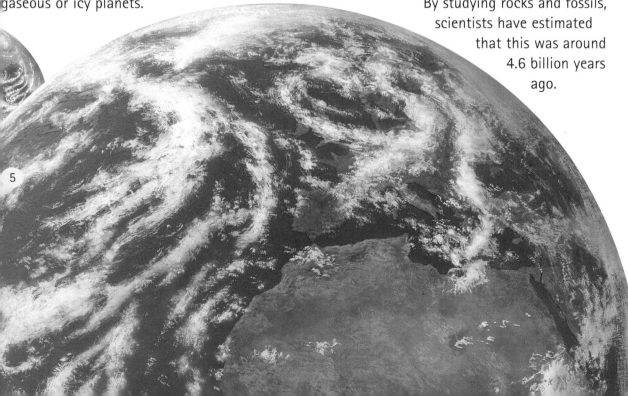

5

Crust to Core

Explorers have charted the continents and oceans of Earth's surface, and satellites beam back detailed pictures of our planet from space. But geologists—scientists who study Earth—seek to understand what lies beneath the surface and to discover what Earth is made of.

Crust

Mantle

Outer core

Inner core

What is Earth made of?

It is about 4,000 miles (6,440km) from the surface of Earth to its center. Earth is made up of different layers of rock and metal. There are three main zones—the outer crust, the mantle below, and the core at the center. The rocky outer crust is divided into two parts—continental crust and oceanic crust. The mantle, which lies beneath the crust, is a layer of molten rock about 1,800 miles (2,800km) thick. Earth's core consists mainly of the metals nickel and iron. It is hot and dense and is divided into two areas—a liquid outer core and a solid inner core.

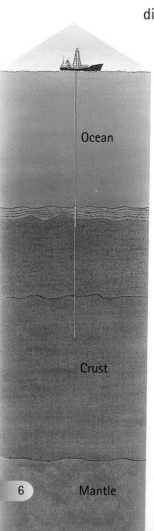

Ocean

Crust

Mantle

How do we know what is inside Earth?

Geologists cannot be absolutely certain what the inside of Earth is like, but they can discover a lot from examining the rocks spewed out from volcanoes. They can also use seismic waves from both earthquakes and nuclear bomb tests to build a three-dimensional picture of the planet. Seismic waves move quickly through hard, dense rock and more slowly through soft rock. In the 1960s scientists tried to drill through the oceanic crust to the mantle (left), but failed because the project was too expensive.

EARTH DATA

Age: 4.6 billion years
Mass: 6.6 sextillion tons
Circumference (distance around Earth at equator): 24,902 miles
Distance from surface to center: 4,000 miles
Temperature at center: 9,000°F

How does Earth aid navigation?

As Earth spins in space electric currents below the surface cause it to act like a magnet. Like a bar magnet, Earth has north and south magnetic poles and a magnetic field. A magnetized needle floating in a bowl of water will align itself with Earth's magnetic poles, creating a simple compass. Some animals, such as pigeons and dolphins, also use Earth's magnetic field to navigate.

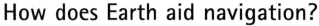

Is Earth round?

From space, Earth looks spherical. However, it is not perfectly round. In fact, it is slightly flatter at the top and the bottom—the poles—and it bulges slightly at the middle, around the equator.

How high is the sky?

The sky, or atmosphere, that surrounds Earth contains a mixture of gases that makes life on the planet possible. The atmosphere is made up of several layers and reaches about 1,000 miles (1,600km) into space. The troposphere, the lowest layer, contains enough air for plants and animals to breathe. The air in the stratosphere is much thinner and contains a thin layer of ozone—a type of oxygen gas that warms the atmosphere and absorbs harmful rays from the sun. The other layers in the atmosphere are the mesosphere, the ionosphere, and the exosphere.

Exosphere

Ionosphere

Mesosphere

Stratosphere

Troposphere

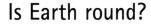
Ozone layer

Water

From space, Earth looks blue. This is because 71 percent of the surface of the planet is covered by water. About 97 percent of the planet's water is salty seawater. The remaining water is in rivers, lakes, and glaciers.

Pacific Ocean

In which sea is it easy to float?

Seawater contains common salt and other minerals. On average, the sea is 3.5 percent salt. However, the Dead Sea, an inland sea, is 25 percent salt. High salt content gives water great buoyancy, so it is very easy for swimmers to float in the Dead Sea.

Which is the biggest ocean?

Oceans are huge bodies of salt water. There are four oceans—the Pacific, the Atlantic, the Indian, and the Arctic. The Pacific is the largest and the deepest. It is more than twice as big as the second-largest ocean, the Atlantic. The Pacific is wide enough to fit all the continents and deep enough to swallow Mount Everest, the world's highest mountain.

Water falls as snow in mountainous areas

Water is transferred inland as clouds move with winds

Plants give off water in a process called transpiration

Water evaporates from lakes and rivers as it flows back into oceans

What is the water cycle?

The world's water is constantly being recycled (above). Rain falls on the land and into the oceans. The sun's rays heat Earth, causing water to evaporate back into the atmosphere. As the water in the atmosphere cools, it condenses to form rain clouds.

Mediterranean Sea

Nile River

Which is the world's longest river?

The longest river in the world is the Nile in Africa (left). It runs 4,157 miles (6,693km) from its source in Lake Victoria, Burundi, to the Mediterranean Sea. Rivers not only play an important role in shaping the landscape, they are also a vital resource for humans, providing food and water for drinking and irrigation. The Nile is so long that it is even visible from space!

How do lakes form?

Lakes can form in a variety of ways. Oxbow lakes are formed when a loop of a winding, or meandering, river gets cut off from the river. Volcanic lakes form in the natural hollows of old volcanoes. Lakes can also form in rift valleys, which occur when the land between two faults—fractures in Earth's crust—slips away.

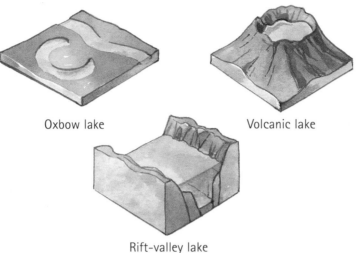

Oxbow lake

Volcanic lake

Rift-valley lake

What causes waves and tides?

As wind blows over the ocean's surface, friction between the air and the water causes wavelets on the surface. These grow bigger, creating waves with high points, or crests, that are separated by low points, or troughs. Tides are caused by Earth's spin and the gravitational pulls of the moon and the sun.

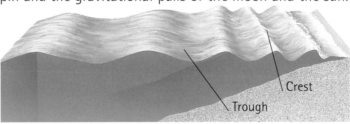

Crest

Trough

Water falls as rain on oceans

Water evaporates from oceans

What is the difference between seas and oceans?

Seas are sections of oceans, but are partly cut off from them by land. The largest sea, the South China Sea, is part of the Pacific Ocean. Most seas and oceans are rich in marine life and mineral resources.

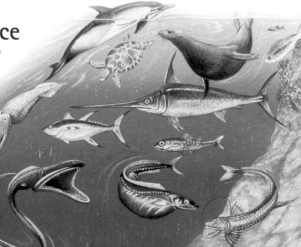

Land

Earth's crust is divided into sections called plates that are moved by the mantle over millions of years. Continental crust—crust that makes up Earth's land—is 19 to 25 miles (30–40km) thick.

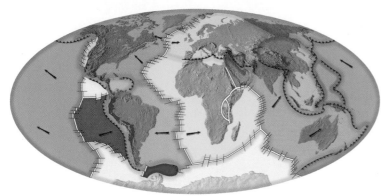

The different colors represent the tectonic plates of Earth's crust. The arrows indicate the direction each plate is moving.

What are tectonic plates?

The surface of Earth is made up of about 20 tectonic plates (above) that move slowly over Earth's surface, causing continents to collide and split apart. Areas where plates pull apart from each other are called divergence zones. Areas where plates push against each other are called convergence zones.

How has Earth changed?

1 About 200 million years ago all the continents were joined together in one giant land mass called Pangaea.

2 By about 130 million years ago Pangaea had split into a northern continent called Laurasia and a southern continent called Gondwanaland.

3 By about 65 million years ago Gondwanaland had split into Africa and South America, and Laurasia was splitting into North America and Eurasia.

4 About 65 million years from now it is likely that North America will split from South America to join Asia. It is also likely that Africa will group closely together with Europe.

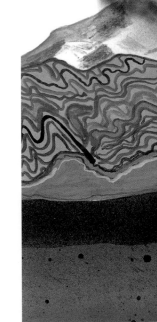

North and South America

Africa

What evidence of plate movement is there?

The shapes of the eastern coast of North and South America and the western coasts of Europe and Africa suggest that they were once joined. Also, scientists have found similarities between rocks, fossils, plants, and animals from different continents—African ostriches and South American rheas probably share an ancestor.

How many continents are there?

There are seven continents—North America, South America, Africa, Asia, Europe, Antarctica, and Australasia. Europe, which is attached to Asia, is the smallest continent, and it is argued that it is really part of Asia. Australasia is made up of Australia, New Zealand, and other Pacific Islands. India is called a subcontinent of Asia because it is so large and distinct.

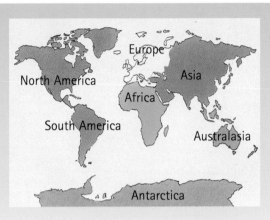

How else have tectonic plates shaped the world?

Plate movement has not only mapped out our continents, but it has also created many geographical features. Mountains are formed when plates crumple land as they collide, and volcanoes erupt when plates dive under the mantle and melt or split apart (below). Earthquakes occur where tectonic plates move past each other.

Are the continents still moving?

Yes. North America and Europe are estimated to be moving 3 inches (7cm) farther apart every year. This means that the Atlantic Ocean is getting wider and the Pacific Ocean is getting smaller.

Quick-fire Quiz

1. Which is the smallest continent?
a) Antarctica
b) Europe
c) Asia

2. What are areas where tectonic plates pull apart called?
a) Convergence zones
b) Divergence zones
c) Continental zones

3. How thick are continental land masses?
a) 9 to 20 miles
b) 19 to 25 miles
c) 29 to 35 miles

4. Which ocean is getting smaller?
a) The Atlantic Ocean
b) The Indian Ocean
c) The Pacific Ocean

Earthquakes

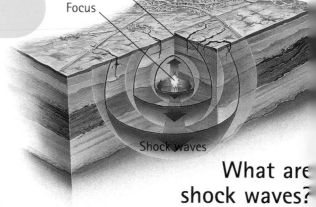

Epicenter
Focus
Shock waves

Earthquakes can be devastating natural disasters. More than a million earthquakes are detected each year, but only a fraction of them are strong enough to cause damage.

What is a fault line?

When plates of continental and oceanic crust slide and push against each other, they cause rocks to snap, forming a line of weakness called a fault. Earthquakes occur along these fault lines. The San Andreas Fault (right), which runs down the western coast of North America, is one of the biggest fault lines in the world. In 1906 a catastrophic earthquake along this fault caused 500 deaths in San Francisco.

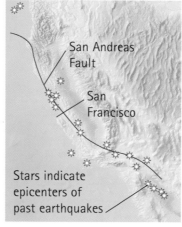

San Andreas Fault

San Francisco

Stars indicate epicenters of past earthquakes

What are shock waves?

Shock waves are waves of energy caused by earthquakes. The source of the waves is called the focus of the quake, and the point on the surface above the focus is referred to as the epicenter. There are two kinds of shock waves. Body waves travel through the rock below the surface, causing it to compress, expand, and move up and down. Surface waves reach Earth's surface and have a rolling motion, just like ocean waves. Usually an earthquake causes the most damage in areas closest to the epicenter.

How are earthquakes caused?

When Earth's plates push against each other, they place enormous stress on rocks near the top of the crust. Instead of rubbing smoothly past each other, they may lock together for years until the pent-up energy is finally released. This causes an earthquake, sending shock waves through the rocks.

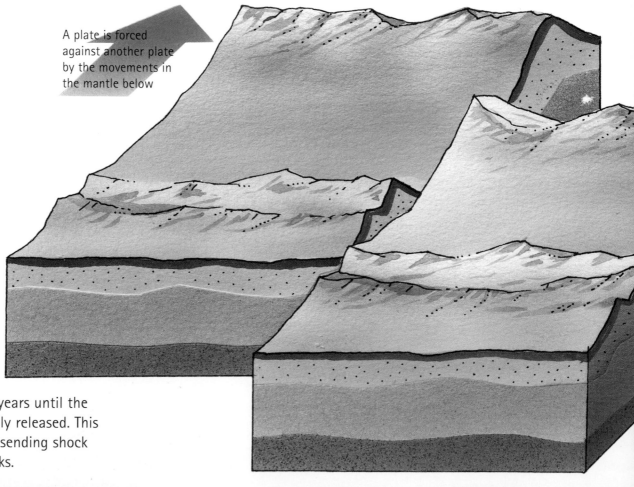

A plate is forced against another plate by the movements in the mantle below

What is a tsunami?

When an earthquake happens beneath the sea, it can create enormous tidal waves called tsunamis. Tsunamis can reach heights of 100 feet (30m) or more by the time they reach coastlines and can cause huge amounts of damage.

What should you do in an earthquake?

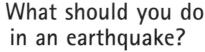

Probably the greatest danger in an earthquake is that a building will collapse on top of you. Standing in a doorway or taking shelter under a table could save your life. Architects and engineers try to construct buildings that resist collapse (left). These buildings have deep foundations in solid rock and are able to bend slightly.

Trans-America Pyramid, San Francisco, CA

Quick-fire Quiz

1. Which fault line is on the western coast of North America?
   a) The San Andreas Fault
   b) The San Francisco Fault
   c) The Great American Fault

2. Where does most of an earthquake's damage usually occur?
   a) Under the ground
   b) In space
   c) At the epicenter

3. What is probably the greatest danger in an earthquake?
   a) Collapsing buildings
   b) Electric shocks
   c) Molten lava

4. Which type of damage would an earthquake measuring 7.1 on the Richter scale cause?
   a) Feeble
   b) Disastrous
   c) Catastrophic

How are earthquakes measured?

Earthquakes are recorded by machines called seismographs (below) and are measured on two scales. The Mercalli Scale is based on the effects of earthquakes. The Richter Scale is based on the size of shock waves.

Mercalli Scale	Ricter Scale
1 Very slight: detected by instruments	less than 3
2 Feeble: felt by people resting	3–3.4
3 Slight: like heavy trucks passing	3.5–4
4 Moderate: windows rattle	4.1–4.4
5 Rather strong: wakes sleeping people	4.5–4.8
6 Strong: trees sway, walls crack	4.9–5.4
7 Very strong: buildings crack	5.5–6
8 Destructive: buildings move	6.1–6.5
9 Ruinous: ground cracks	6.6–7
10 Disastrous: landslides	7.1–7.3
11 Very disastrous: railroad tracks break	7.4–8.1
12 Catastrophic: total devastation	8.1 and over

What damage can earthquakes cause?

Depending on the strength of the earthquake, areas can be completely devastated. The ground shakes and ripples, and huge cracks open up. Buildings collapse, and electricity lines, water mains, and gas pipes are destroyed. Fires often start, causing further chaos. Some earthquakes have caused the deaths of thousands of people. Approximately 30,000 people were killed by an earthquake in northern Turkey in August 1999.

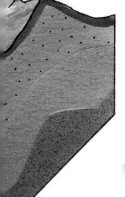

As the plates attempt to move past each other, tension builds up and will be released in the form of an earthquake

Mountains

Formed over millions of years, mountains create some of the world's most dramatic landscapes. Most occur in ranges that stretch for hundreds of miles. Many of these ranges will continue to grow up before erosion eventually reduces them to the size of hills.

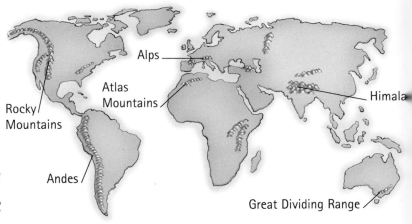

Alps
Atlas Mountains
Rocky Mountains
Himala...
Andes
Great Dividing Range

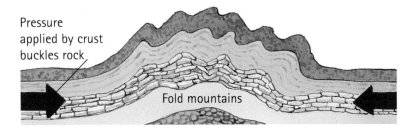

Pressure applied by crust buckles rock

Fold mountains

How are mountains formed?

Volcanic mountains are formed when molten rock escapes through cracks in Earth's crust and builds up on the surface. Block mountains occur when a chunk of land is thrust above neighboring rock along fault lines in Earth's crust. The mountains in the great ranges are fold mountains. They are formed when two slabs of continental crust collide, buckling the rock and sediment between them (above). The Himalayas were formed in this way (right).

India hits Asia, crumpling both continental crusts and forming the Himalayan mountain range

Where are mountains found?

Mountains can be found all over the world (above). The greatest mountain ranges are the Rockies in North America, the Alps in Europe, the Andes in South America and the highest of them all—the Himalayas in Asia.

How do mountains stay upright?

It is thought that Earth's crust "floats" on the mantle below. Mountains have "roots" that reach deep below ground level and support them.

What life can be found on mountains?

Animals and plants that live on mountains have to be able to survive extreme temperatures and high winds. Trees are unable to survive above a certain altitude known as the tree line. However, hardy alpine plants can grow higher up. Mountain animals such as llamas, yaks, goats, and hares have thick, woolly coats to keep out the cold.

Why are some mountains rugged and others smooth?

Young mountains, such as the Himalayas, have steep, rugged peaks and sides. Over time the peaks and sides will be eroded by water, rain, ice, and wind. This makes older mountains smoother and less high.

Which is the highest mountain?

The world's highest peak is Mount Everest (below). It is part of the Himalayas in Asia and is 29,021 feet (8,848m) high. On May 29, 1953, New Zealand mountaineer Edmund Hillary and his Sherpa guide, Tenzing Norgay (right), made history by reaching the summit of Everest. Mauna Kea in Hawaii is 33,476 feet (10,203m) high. However, 19,680 feet (5,998m) of the mountain lies beneath the ocean.

Edmund Hillary and
Tenzing Norgay

Quick-fire Quiz

1. Which mountain range is found in South America?
a) The Alps
b) The Rockies
c) The Andes

2. Which type of mountains are in the great ranges?
a) Volcanic mountains
b) Fold mountains
c) Block mountains

3. What is the line above which trees are unable to grow called?
a) The tree line
b) The growth line
c) The altitude line

4. How high is Mauna Kea?
a) 3,476 feet
b) 23,476 feet
c) 33,476 feet

Volcanoes

An erupting volcano spewing hot, molten rock is one of the most dramatic sights on Earth. Volcanic eruptions are caused by disturbances in Earth's crust. There are about 500 active volcanoes in the world.

What are volcanoes?

Volcanoes are openings in Earth's crust from which hot, molten rock (magma), ash, and gas spurt. The magma, which is called lava after eruption, cools around the openings to form cone shapes. Volcanoes often occur in mountain ranges on land, but they can also form on ocean floors, rising above sea level (above).

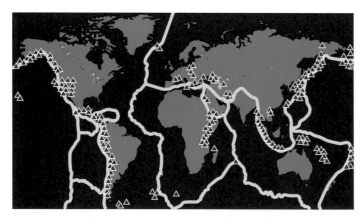

Pink triangles show active volcanoes. Plate boundaries are in yellow.

Where are volcanoes found?

Most of Earth's volcanoes are located along plate boundaries (above), where tectonic plates meet, because this is where crust is weakest. There are so many volcanoes surrounding the Pacific Ocean that it is known as the Ring of Fire. A few volcanoes occur away from plate edges, above "hot spots"—areas where Earth's crust is thin and magma can burn through. Some islands are the tops of volcanoes that have emerged from the ocean floor. The Hawaiian Islands are examples of this.

Magma chamber

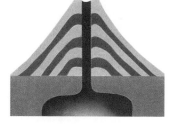
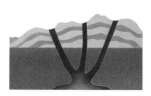

Cinder-cone volcano   Composite volcano   Shield volcano

Are there different types of volcanoes?

A volcano's shape depends on how thick the magma is and the force with which it is spewed out. A cinder cone is formed after a huge explosion, which occurs if there is a lot of gas in the magma. The cone of the volcano is made mostly of volcanic ash. A composite volcano erupts regularly and is usually very tall, made of alternating layers of lava and ash. The lava is thick and sticky and does not flow far before it solidifies. A shield volcano has several craters and is formed when magma is thin and runny. It spreads across a wide area to form a low dome shape.

What are geysers?

Geysers are found in volcanic areas where hot rocks lie near Earth's surface. Underground water is heated to boiling point by the rocks, then shoots into the air in a fountain. In New Zealand and Iceland the power from geysers and hot springs is used to make electricity. One of the world's most famous geysers is Old Faithful in Yellowstone National Park, which shoots up a jet of water and steam every 70 minutes.

Quick-fire Quiz

1. What is hot, molten rock called?
a) Volcanic ash
b) Red-hot rock
c) Lava or magma

2. Where is the Ring of Fire?
a) The Pacific Ocean
b) The Atlantic Ocean
c) North America

3. Which type of volcano is formed by runny lava?
a) A shield volcano
b) A cinder volcano
c) A composite volcano

4. How often does Old Faithful erupt?
a) Every 70 minutes
b) Every 70 hours
c) Every 70 days

What happens when a volcano erupts?

Deep beneath a volcano lies a magma chamber (left). Pressure builds up inside the chamber, and the magma escapes through a chimneylike vent. During an eruption rock and ash are spewed out with the magma.

What is a dormant volcano?

A dormant volcano is a volcano that has been quiet for hundreds of years. However, there is always a danger that a dormant volcano may suddenly erupt. A volcano that has permanently stopped erupting is said to be extinct.

Rocks, Fossils, and Minerals

Earth's many varied landscapes are all shaped out of rock. There are three main types of rock—igneous, metamorphic, and sedimentary—and they are all formed in different ways.

Amethyst

What are minerals?

All rocks are made up o building blocks called minerals Minerals are natural chemica compounds, and nearly al consist of just eight chemica elements—oxygen, silicon calcium, magnesium, potassium aluminum, iron, and sodium When minerals are cut anc polished and are considered to be beautiful and durable enough to wear as jewelry, they are known as gemstones or gems (left). Gems are valued according to thei hardness, density, color, anc how they reflect light

Opal

Diamond

Ruby

Emerald

What are "fiery" rocks?

After molten magma forces its way through cracks in Earth's crust, it gradually cools, forms crystals, and becomes a hard mass of igneous rock. The word "igneous" comes from the Latin word for fire. Granite (left) and basalt are examples of igneous rock.

Granite

What is metamorphic rock?

Metamorphic rock is igneous or sedimentary rock that has been changed by great heat or pressure. For example, magma under the ground can bake surrounding limestone and change it into marble. The forces that build new mountains also create metamorphic rock, changing soft mudstone into hard slate (left).

Slate

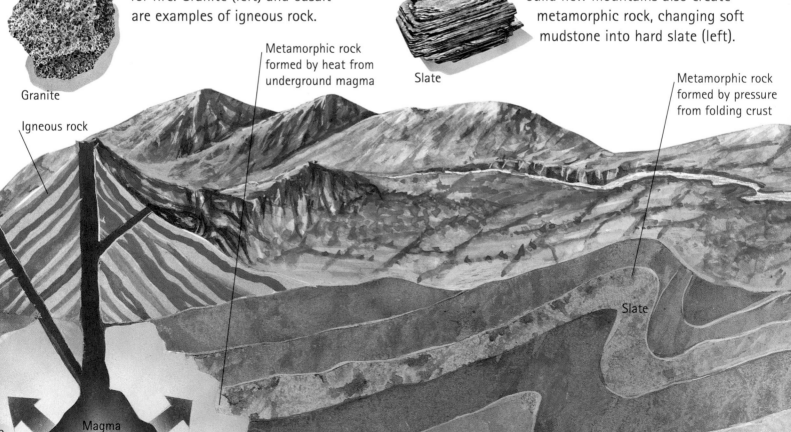

Metamorphic rock formed by heat from underground magma

Metamorphic rock formed by pressure from folding crust

Igneous rock

Slate

Magma chamber

Marble

How do fossils form?

Fossils are the remains of animals and plants that lived more than 10,000 years ago. Most fossils are formed in sedimentary rock.

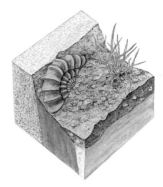

1 When a sea animal such as an ammonite dies, its body sinks to the seabed. The soft parts rot away, leaving the hard shell.

2 The shell is buried under more and more sediment. Over time this sediment hardens into rock.

3 Over millions of years the rock in which the fossil lies may shift, and the fossil could be thrust up to become part of a new mountain range.

4 Eventually the effects of weathering and erosion wear away the rock and expose the fossil.

How is limestone formed?

Limestone is a sedimentary rock. All sedimentary rock is made from sediments such as shells, sand, and mud that settle on the bottom of seas, lakes, and rivers. Sediments pile up in layers, and pressure from the higher layers squeezes water out from the lower layers. The squashed sediments cement together to form solid rock. Limestone is formed from the shells and skeletons of tiny sea creatures. Sandstone and chalk (right) are also sedimentary rocks.

Chalk

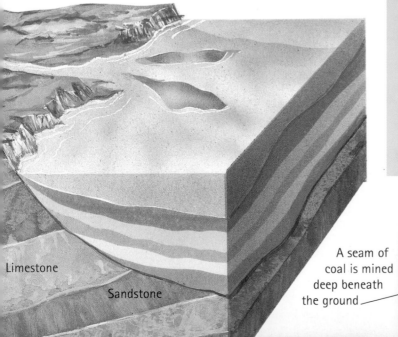

Limestone

Sandstone

What use are rocks, fossils, and minerals?

Rocks are used as building materials, and some minerals are useful in industry—silicon is used to make glass, and diamonds make good cutting tools (some drills are tipped with diamonds). Coal, a fossil fuel, is mined from deep underground (below). It is the remains of prehistoric plants that built up in thick layers. The layers were flooded by the sea and covered with sand, which over millions of years compressed the layers into coal.

A seam of coal is mined deep beneath the ground

Quick-fire Quiz

1. Which type of rock is granite?
a) Igneous
b) Sedimentary
c) Metamorphic

2. Which of these is a sedimentary rock?
a) Chalk
b) Basalt
c) Marble

3. Which metamorphic rock can limestone be changed into?
a) Slate
b) Granite
c) Marble

4. In which type of rock are fossils usually found?
a) Igneous
b) Sedimentary
c) Metamorphic

Climate

Climate is the average weather conditions of a region, season by season. Many factors affect climate—global position, ocean currents, and the greenhouse effect. As these factors continue to change, so too will Earth's climate.

Spring in NH

Fall in SH

Summer in NH

Winter in SH

Sun

Winter in NH

Summer in SH

Fall in NH

Spring in SH

Key
NH Northern Hemisphere
SH Southern Hemisphere

Why does Earth have seasons?

Earth has seasons because its axis tilts, so as it orbits the sun, one hemisphere is always tipped closer to the sun than the other hemisphere is. When the Northern Hemisphere is closer to the sun—from March 21 to September 20—it will experience spring and summer, while the Southern Hemisphere will be in fall and winter. When the Southern Hemisphere is closer to the sun—from September 21 to March 20—it will have spring and summer, while the Northern Hemisphere will experience its fall and winter.

Why are some places hotter than others?

Different parts of the world have different temperatures. Because Earth is round, the sun does not heat it evenly (below). Areas near the equator have a hot climate year-round because the sun is directly overhead. Farther away from the equator, the sun's rays are spread over a much larger area, so it is not as hot. Although equatorial regions do not experience much change in temperature, they do have rainy and dry seasons.

Sun's rays spread over very large area—cold at North Pole

Sun's rays spread over large area—warm

Sun's rays directed at small area—hot at equator

Equator

Warm

Cold at South Pole

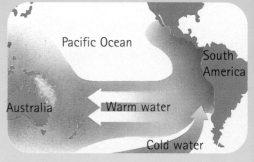

Pacific Ocean

South America

Australia

Warm water

Cold water

How do ocean currents affect climates?

Ocean currents bring warm or cold water to continental coasts. This water heats or cools air masses, and this affects the climate in the local area. Warm currents move west across the Pacific (above), providing southeastern Asia and northern Australia with a warm, humid climate.

Climate zones of the world

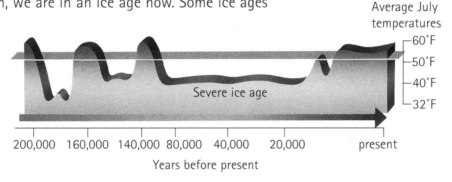

- ☐ Polar
- ☐ Cold
- ☐ Temperate
- ☐ Arid
- ☐ Tropical

How does global position affect climate?

Climate depends on many geographical factors—mountainous areas are cold, and places close to the ocean are wetter than inland regions. Global position also affects climate (left). Polar regions are snowy and icy, and even areas with simply "cold" climates may be frozen for months on end. Temperate climates have warm summers, cool winters, and rain. Arid desert areas are hot and dry, and tropical areas are hot and wet.

What is an ice age?

An ice age is a period when part of Earth is permanently covered by ice. Because the poles are frozen, we are in an ice age now. Some ice ages are more severe than others—millions of years ago ice sheets covered most of Earth during ice ages. The last severe ice age took place between about 20,000 and 80,000 years ago (right).

Average July temperatures

- 60°F
- 50°F
- 40°F
- 32°F

Severe ice age

200,000 160,000 140,000 80,000 40,000 20,000 present

Years before present

What is the greenhouse effect?

Some of the sun's heat is not absorbed by Earth and is reflected back into space. Gases in Earth's atmosphere, such as carbon dioxide, nitrogen oxide, and chlorofluorocarbons (CFCs), trap some of this heat and radiate it back to Earth. This is the greenhouse effect. Without the greenhouse effect, it would be too cold on Earth for life to exist. However, too many CFCs, which are released by industry, have entered the atmosphere, and this is causing too much heat to be trapped. This causes excessive global warming, which is harmful and alters Earth's climate over time.

Sun's heat enters atmosphere

Some radiated heat escapes

Sun's heat reflected back into space

Radiated heat trapped in atmosphere causes global warming

Weather

Weather is the day-to-day changes in atmospheric conditions—sunshine, rainfall, and wind speeds. Some areas have similar weather every day, while others have very changeable weather.

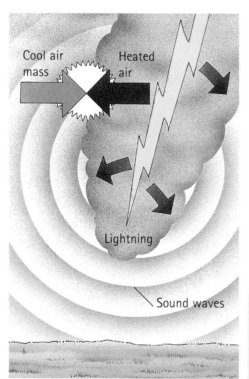

Cool air mass

Heated air

Lightning

Sound waves

What are thunder and lightning?

In a storm cloud, air currents force water droplets to crash into each other until they become electrically charged. Lightning is the huge spark of electricity produced as the charge is released. Lightning heats the air around it so quickly that it produces a loud, booming noise—thunder (above). To work out how far away a storm is, count the seconds between the lightning and thunder—five seconds indicates one mile (1.6km).

Why does it snow?

Tiny water droplets in cloud freeze to form ice crystals. These six-sided crystals can bind together and create beautiful snowflakes (left). The ice crystals are heavy, so they will fall from the clouds. If the temperature of the air below the clouds is less than 32°F (0°C), the ice crystals will remain frozen and fall as snow. If the air is above 32°F (0°C), the ice crystals will melt and fall as rain.

How are clouds made?

Water vapor in the air condenses into tiny droplets. The droplets are not heavy enough to fall as rain, and instead they group together to form clouds. Different conditions form clouds of different types and shapes (below). Cirrocumulus clouds look like ripples. Altocumulus clouds are white and puffy. Cumulus clouds are big, cauliflower-shaped clouds. Stratus clouds are flat and low-lying.

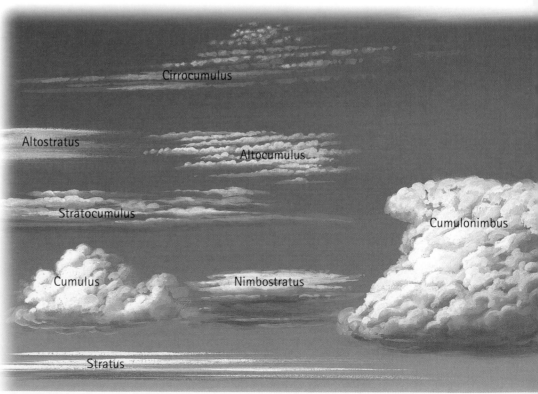

Cirrocumulus

Altostratus

Altocumulus

Stratocumulus

Cumulonimbus

Cumulus

Nimbostratus

Stratus

How are rainbows caused?

Rainbows, which appear in the sky after rain, are the reflection of sunlight in raindrops. The raindrops split the sunlight into a spectrum of colors— red, orange, yellow, green, blue, indigo, and violet (right). To see a rainbow, your back must be to the sun.

How is weather forecast?

The science of studying weather systems is called meteorology. Information on temperature, cloud type, wind speed, air pressure, rain, and snow is collected regularly from places all over the world. In addition to information from the ground, meteorologists can get an accurate picture of the weather from satellites in space (left). The information is sent to forecasting stations and plotted onto charts. Meteorologists can make fairly accurate forecasts up to a week ahead.

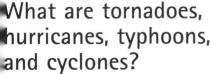
Weather satellite

What are tornadoes, hurricanes, typhoons, and cyclones?

A tornado is a twisting storm funnel about 330 feet (100m) wide. The winds inside the tornado can reach speeds of 220 miles per hour (355km/h). Tornadoes move in straight lines across land and are most common on the Great Plains (right). At the center, or eye, of a tornado is an area of pressure so low that it can cause buildings to explode. Hurricanes are much bigger storms that form over tropical waters in the Atlantic Ocean. They are so powerful that when they strike land, they can devastate crops, forests, and buildings. Storms that form over the Pacific Ocean are called typhoons, and ones that occur over the Indian Ocean are called cyclones.

Quick-fire Quiz

1. Which clouds are flat and low-lying?
   a) Cirrus
   b) Stratus
   c) Cumulus

2. What are tropical storms that form over the Pacific Ocean called?
   a) Hurricanes
   b) Typhoons
   c) Cyclones

3. What is the study of weather systems called?
   a) Meteorology
   b) Microbiology
   c) Weatherology

4. What is lightning?
   a) A spark of electricity
   b) Crashing air currents
   c) Loud, booming noises

Polar Regions

The North and South poles are at the north and south points of Earth's axis. The polar regions of the Arctic (north) and Antarctica (south) are the coldest areas on Earth (below). Ice and snow stretch as far as the eye can see.

Arctic

Antarctica

Do any people live in Antarctica?

Only scientists live in Antarctica, and they normally stay only in the summer months. The land is not owned by any country, and the Antarctic Treaty, now agreed to by more than 40 countries, ensures that the land is used only for research. Tourism is increasing in the area, and waste disposal is a problem—the freezing temperatures preserve waste rather than cause it to decompose.

Is there any land in the Arctic Circle?

There is no land at the North Pole itself—just a mass of pack ice. However, most of Greenland and parts of Canada, Alaska, and Scandinavia lie within the Arctic Circle. Antarctica is a continental land mass covered by an ice sheet.

How cold is Antarctica?

The lowest temperature ever recorded on Earth was –128.2°F (–89.2°C) at Vostok in Antarctica. Temperatures inland range from –13°F (–25°C) to –128°F (–89°C). Ice sheets are up to 9,840 feet (3km) thick, and the ice and snow reflect the sun's heat back into space. Icy winds can blow at speeds of up to 90 miles per hour (145km/h). It has not rained in Antarctica for two million years.

What are icebergs?

Icebergs are parts of the Arctic and Antarctic ice sheets that have broken off into the ocean. Icebergs vary in size and shape, and some can be the size of a small country. As much as 90 percent of an iceberg is underwater. This is why they are hazardous to ships, which are often unable to detect them.

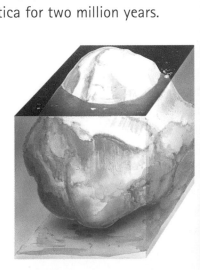

What are glaciers?

A glacier is a large body of ice that moves slowly through mountain valleys and polar regions. Glaciers move less than seven feet (2m) a day, but they are so big that they can dramatically shape and carve the land they pass through. During the past ice ages, much of Europe, North America, South Africa, and Asia was covered by glaciers. When glaciers meet the ocean, chunks can break off into the sea and form icebergs (below).

Quick-fire Quiz

1. Where is the South Pole?
a) The Arctic
b) Antarctica
c) Greenland

2. Where are polar bears found?
a) The Arctic
b) Antarctica
c) Australia

3. How far do glaciers move each day?
a) Less than 7 feet
b) 7 to 15 feet
c) 15 to 27 feet

4. Which country lies within the Arctic Circle?
a) Ireland
b) Iceland
c) Greenland

What is tundra?

Tundra (above) is the land around the Arctic Circle between the northern conifer forests and the permanent ice sheets around the North Pole. The surface soil in the tundra thaws for only a few weeks in the summer, but below the surface the ground is permanently frozen. This means that vegetation cannot extend its roots very deep, and only small shrubs, mosses, and trees can grow there.

How do animals survive in polar climates?

Polar animals have thick coats or layers of fat (blubber) to keep warm. Polar mammals usually have small ears and snouts to avoid losing too much heat. Penguins, whales, seals, and seabirds fish in the icy seas, and musk oxen graze on plants in the tundra, where they live all year round. Polar bears live only in the Arctic, and penguins live only in Antarctica.

Arctic tern

Penguins   Seal   Musk ox   Polar bear

Deserts

Deserts are regions where the annual rainfall is less than 10 inches (25cm), but some deserts have no rain for several years. Deserts are the driest places on Earth and are often very windy. Few plants can survive in these conditions.

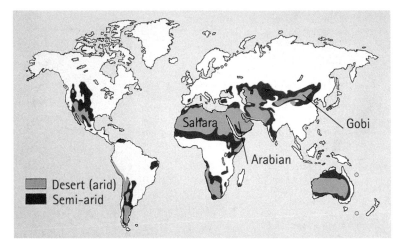

Desert (arid)
Semi-arid

Which are the largest deserts?

The three largest deserts in the world are the Sahara, the Arabian, and the Gobi (above). The Sahara covers about one third of Africa, measuring about 3,354,000 square miles (8,600,000km²). The Arabian Desert and the Gobi Desert in Asia measure 897,000 square miles (2,300,000km²) and 468,000 square miles (1,200,000km²), respectively. Australia has several deserts that cover a huge area of land.

Wind direction

Dunes "migrate" in direction of wind

How are dunes formed?

Many deserts have sandy mounds called dunes. Dunes are formed when the wind blows steadily from one direction. Sand grains lodge against stones or bushes, and over time the sand piles up, forming dunes. Whole dunes are moved along by the wind as sand on the gently inclined, wind-facing side of the dune is swept over the top of the dune (above). Dunes shaped like crescent moons are called barchan dunes.

Are deserts always hot?

Daytime temperatures can rise to a scorching 122°F (50°C) in some deserts. Once the sun sets, however, temperatures can drop dramatically, because there are few clouds over deserts to keep the day's heat in. Day and night temperatures in the western Sahara can differ by more than 113°F (45°C); the Gobi has a more temperate climate. Many people consider the polar regions to be cold deserts because they have no rain.

Are all deserts sandy?

Most deserts are rocky, not sandy. Only about 11 percent of the Sahara is sandy. Many deserts contain huge, strangely shaped rocks that have been formed by wind erosion.

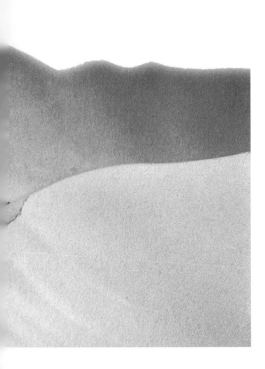

What is an oasis?

Deserts are very dry places. An oasis (above) is a small fertile area in a desert where water from under the ground reaches the surface. Many oases occur naturally, although they can be created artificially by digging wells in places where water lies close to the surface. Plants can grow near oases, but elsewhere some plants lie dormant and wait for rain.

Can people live in deserts?

Many people who live in deserts are nomads who wander from place to place in search of food and water. Permanent settlements are formed around oases, and because it is now possible to make artificial oases, more and more people are now living in desert lands.

What life is found in deserts?

Many desert animals, such as foxes, jackrabbits, and coyotes, are nocturnal, sleeping during the scorching hot day and coming out to find food at night, when it is cooler. Some desert animals are able to survive with little or no water—camels can go for many days without drinking. Desert plants store water in their fleshy stems and leaves. Cacti swell after rain and gradually get thinner as they use the water.

Grasslands

Grasslands lie just beyond the edges of deserts and in the dry interiors of continents. In these regions rain falls during only one season of the year. The land is too dry to support many trees, but drought-resistant grasses flourish.

Why are grasslands good for grazing?

Large areas of the grasslands of North America, South America, Australia, and New Zealand are used to graze sheep or cattle (left). Because grass leaves grow from the base of the plant, they can survive and grow even if the tops of the plant are eaten. This makes grassland areas ideal for ranches, which rear livestock. Grasslands are also used to grow food crops like wheat and corn.

Where are grasslands found?

Grasslands are found all over the world, in the dry central areas of continents and on the edges of deserts (below). The grassland of Europe and Asia is called "steppe." In South America it is called "pampas," and in North America it is "prairie." The grasslands of Africa, India, and Australia are called "savanna." There are more than 8,000 different species of grasses around the world.

Prairie

Steppe

Savanna

Pampas

Savanna

Grasslands of the world

When were the prairies a "Dust Bowl"?

The grassland climate is very dry, and long droughts are common. In the 1930s a severe drought hit the prairies of the central United States. Overgrazing and poor farming reduced the ground to dust, and strong winds brought dust storms to the region. The area became known as the "Dust Bowl."

Which animals live in grasslands?

The animal species found in grasslands vary from continent to continent. The prairies of North America (left) were once home to buffalo, and they are still the habitat of falcons, coyotes, and prairie dogs. Kangaroos, koalas, emus, and kookaburras live in the Australian savanna. The savanna of Africa (below) shelters a rich variety of wildlife—from elephants and giraffes to lions and antelopes.

What is "slash-and-burn"?

Because grassland is useful for growing crops and grazing livestock, humans have looked for ways to extend it. Setting fire to vegetation during the dry season destroys woody plants and encourages new growth. The process is called "slash-and-burn."

Forests

Forests are huge areas of land covered with trees. There are many types of forests—coniferous, deciduous, and the spectacular tropical rain forests. A huge variety of wildlife and vegetation can be found deep within forests.

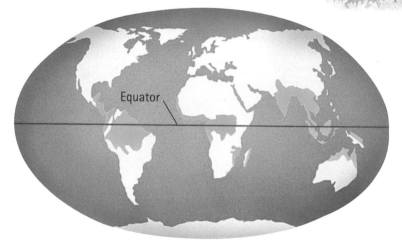

Rain forests of the world

How often does it rain in a rain forest?

Rain forests, or jungles, grow near the equator (above), where temperatures are high and the air is moist—it rains nearly every day. The conditions are ideal for wildlife. In fact, about half the world's plant and animal species are found in rain forests.

What is the rain forest's canopy?

There are several different levels in a rain forest. The forest floor is home to shrubs, climbing plants, moss, and fungi. It is very dark, and the floor is covered with decaying leaves and plants. The canopy (above) is the top of thousands of mature trees. It forms a kind of roof over the rain forest. Many forest animals, such as brightly colored birds and monkeys, live in it. Above the canopy a few taller trees break through, providing homes for big birds of prey.

How do rain forests help us breathe?

Rain forests play a vital role in Earth's oxygen cycle. The mass of vegetation in the vast rain forests takes in enormous amounts of carbon dioxide. The carbon dioxide is converted by the plants into oxygen, which is returned to Earth's atmosphere. This is one of the reasons why environmentalists are determined to halt the destruction of rain forests.

How do forest fires start?

Forest fires may be started by lightning, arson, or even the sun's rays magnified through an empty glass bottle. Fires often spread very quickly in forests—at speeds of up to 1.25 miles (2km) a minute. Firefighters battle against the huge fires, often helped by airplanes that dump huge loads of water onto the flames. Fires can rage for months, and the damage they cause is enormous—homes are destroyed, and air for thousands of miles around is polluted.

How do humans use forests?

Forests are rich resources for humans. They provide timber, food, and medicines. Timber, which can be burned for heating and cooking, is also used for building and for making products like paper. The sap from rubber trees can be made into rubber tires and gloves. Rain forests provide foods such as coffee, cocoa, nutmeg, and pepper. Many rain forest plants are used to develop medicines—quinine, used to treat malaria, comes from cinchona trees. The rain forests are now under threat of destruction as more and more trees are cut down.

What is the difference between a deciduous and a coniferous forest?

Deciduous trees, such as the oak (left), shed their leaves in winter. An oak tree can house more than 300 animal species. Coniferous trees, such as the fir tree (left), have hard, narrow leaves, or needles, that they keep all year round. For this reason, conifers are known as evergreens. The biggest forest in the world is coniferous. It stretches across northern Asia and Europe. Coniferous forests thrive in cold areas with long winters, while deciduous forests grow in more temperate regions.

Fir tree (coniferous)   Oak tree (deciduous)

What do woodland animals eat?

Deciduous and coniferous forests are found in North America, Europe, and northern Asia. Most animals that live in these woodlands eat leaves and seeds, but some birds eat insects, and some animals eat meat—the wild boar eats mice as well as fungi and acorns. The gray squirrel leaps among the trees in search of fruit and birds' eggs, while deer nibble leaves from the lower branches of trees. Foxes emerge at night to hunt small mammals such as rabbits and mice.

Life on Earth

Simple organisms
3,000 million years ago
(m.y.a.)

Earth is the only planet in the universe that is known to support life. Millions of species of plants and animals currently live in the oceans and on the land, but 95 percent of all species that have ever existed are now extinct.

What is evolution?

Evolution is the way in which the characteristics of living things change over time. According to Darwin's theory of natural selection, only "successful" animals will survive over time—animals with useless characteristics will either adapt or become extinct. Darwin noted that evolution had adapted the beaks of finches on the Galapagos Islands (left) to suit different foods.

Seed-eating   Berry-eating

Insect-eating   Cactus-eating

Charles Darwin

When did life on Earth begin?

Life on Earth began about three billion years ago when chemicals dissolved in the oceans and simple bacteria grew. Then marine plants developed, producing oxygen that enabled marine animals to form. Over time life developed on land.

When did humans first appear?

Modern humans (*homo sapiens sapiens*) probably originated in Africa about 120,000 years ago. When European Neanderthals became extinct about 35,000 years ago, *homo sapiens sapiens* became dominant.

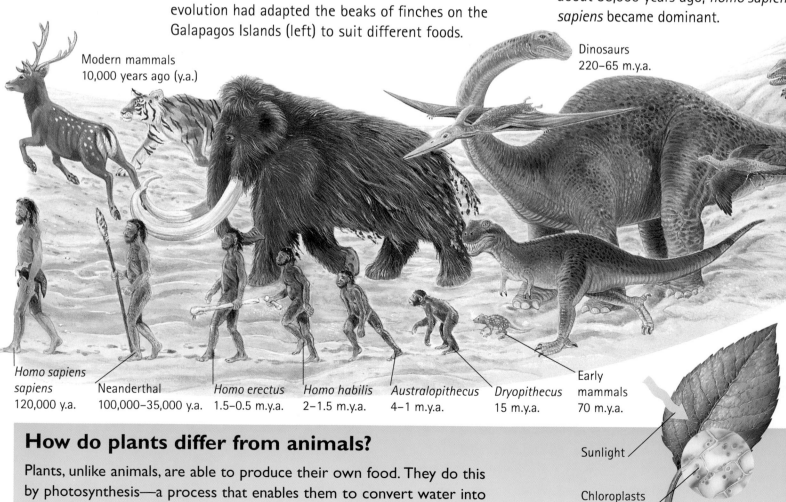

Modern mammals
10,000 years ago (y.a.)

Dinosaurs
220–65 m.y.a.

Homo sapiens
sapiens
120,000 y.a.

Neanderthal
100,000–35,000 y.a.

Homo erectus
1.5–0.5 m.y.a.

Homo habilis
2–1.5 m.y.a.

Australopithecus
4–1 m.y.a.

Dryopithecus
15 m.y.a.

Early
mammals
70 m.y.a.

How do plants differ from animals?

Plants, unlike animals, are able to produce their own food. They do this by photosynthesis—a process that enables them to convert water into energy with the aid of sunlight and natural solar cells, or chloroplasts (right).

Sunlight

Chloroplasts
in leaf cells

Which is the most common type of animal?

Explorers and scientists have discovered more than one million animal species, and 97 percent of these are invertebrates. Invertebrates are animals without backbones, including insects, spiders, jellyfish, worms, and mollusks. Vertebrate species—animals with backbones—include reptiles, birds, fish, amphibians, and mammals.

Marine life
600–375 m.y.a.

Amphibians
375–275 m.y.a.

Reptiles
275 m.y.a.

Do animals always stay in the same habitat?

Many animals migrate to warmer climates to avoid the cold weather and food shortages of winter. The longest migration is that of the Arctic tern, which travels 24,800 miles (40,000km) from the Arctic to Antarctica each year (above). Some animals migrate to reproduce—loggerhead turtles swim up to 1,240 miles (2,000km) to their birthplace, where they lay eggs. Many animals do not migrate, and some are found naturally in only one particular part of the world—kangaroos are found only in Australia, ostriches live only in Africa, and giant anteaters are found only in South America.

Quick-fire Quiz

1. When did life on Earth begin?
a) 300 million years ago
b) 3 billion years ago
c) 30 billion years ago

2. How many animal species have been found?
a) 1 million
b) 5 million
c) 10 million

3. What percentage of animal species is invertebrate?
a) 50 percent
b) 79 percent
c) 97 percent

4. Where do ostriches live?
a) Africa
b) Australia
c) South America

2 Freshwater shrimp and snails eat the plants.

3 Trout feed on the shrimp and snails.

1 Water plants produce energy from sunlight, soil, and water.

What is a food chain?

Living things need energy. Plants, which convert light energy into food, are eaten by insects or other animals, which are then eaten by meat-eaters. When living things die, they rot and release nutrients into the ground. In this way, energy is passed along a food chain. Animals and plants can belong to many different chains. The food web is the interconnection of different chains.

4 An otter preys on the trout.

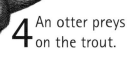

6 Bacteria, flies, and maggots feed on the otter, which returns nutrients to the soil.

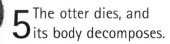

5 The otter dies, and its body decomposes.

33

Human Landscape

Humans have dramatically changed the face of Earth. Farming, industrialization, and the growth of towns and cities have all had a huge impact on the way we live and on the environment.

What is a city?

A city is a large, important town. It has a big population and is usually a center of commerce and industry. Most cities have grown over time from small towns or villages. Today nearly half of the world's population lives in cities, which are often overcrowded. To create more working and living space, many cities have tall buildings called skyscrapers (right).

How many people are there in the world?

In 2007, the world's population was around 6.6 billion. It has grown very quickly—in 1850 it was only about 1.3 billion. Experts predict that by the year 2025 it will have grown by another 3 billion—on average, three people are born every second! Population growth varies from country to country. Poorer countries often have higher birth rates than richer ones. This can cause long-term problems for the poorer countries because they have limited food supplies and resources.

The world's population in 2007

13 billion
12 billion
11 billion
10 billion
9 billion
8 billion
7 billion
6 billion
5 billion
4 billion
3 billion
2 billion
1 billion

1600 1700 1800 1900 2000 2100

Which city has the largest population?

It is not easy to measure city populations. Statistics vary according to how and when populations are counted. Official population counts, or censuses, are carried out every few years and provide the most accurate estimates. Tokyo in Japan probably has the largest population (more than 35 million), and Mexico City has the second largest (19 million). Mumbai (Bombay), India, and São Paulo, Brazil, follow with populations of around 18 million each.

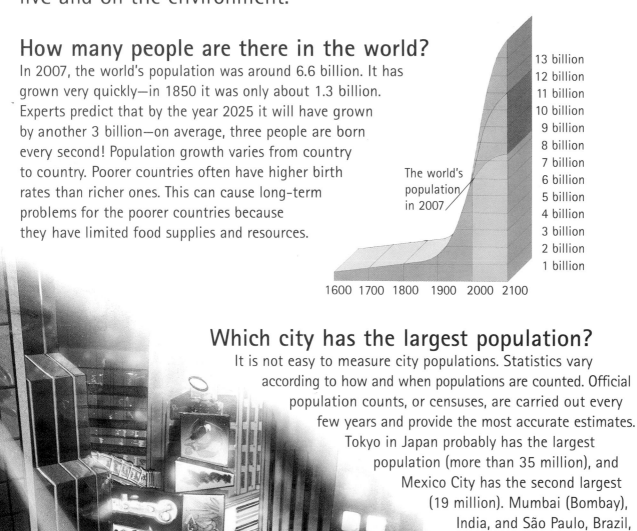

What is a developing country?

A developing country is a nation that has not experienced the development of new technologies and growth in wealth that many richer countries have. Most developing countries are located in the Southern Hemisphere, where extreme climates and lack of resources make progress difficult. Many developing countries have high levels of debt after borrowing money from developed countries and world banking organizations. A nation's wealth is judged by examining its gross national product (GNP)—income generated per year. Developed countries, like Japan, have higher GNPs than developing countries, like India (right).

India

How have changes in farming methods industrialized countries?

The increased use of machinery and improvements in farming methods have resulted in farming being less labor-intensive. This means that fewer farm workers are needed to work the land. In the past most people worked on farms, producing food for hundreds of people, but now many have left the countryside to take jobs in towns and cities. This enables countries to industrialize by developing their industries, factories, and economy. Many people in poorer countries still work in agriculture.

What is an aging population?

In a country with an aging population, the average age of the population is high. This is because the country has a low birth rate—fewer children are born—and because good medical care helps people live longer. Aging populations are usually found in developed countries. Developing countries, where people have more children and shorter life expectancies, have young populations. In Africa nearly 50 percent of the population is under the age of 15.

Quick-fire Quiz

1. What was 2007's estimated world population?
a) 1.3 billion
b) 3 billion
c) 6.6 billion

2. How many people are born every second?
a) One
b) Three
c) Ten

3. What does GNP stand for?
a) General national population
b) Great national possibilities
c) Gross national product

4. Which countries usually have aging populations?
a) Developed countries
b) Developing countries
c) African countries

Earth's Resources

Earth is rich in natural resources that we can use to make energy, goods, and materials. Many of these natural resources are extracted from deep within the ground or from under the ocean.

What is a renewable resource?

A renewable resource is a resource we can use without permanently reducing the amount available to us. Sunlight, wind, and water are all renewable resources, and there are many ways that we can produce energy from them (below). Coal, oil, gas, and wood are nonrenewable resources, and one day they will run out. Scientists believe that gas and oil supplies could run out in a few decades.

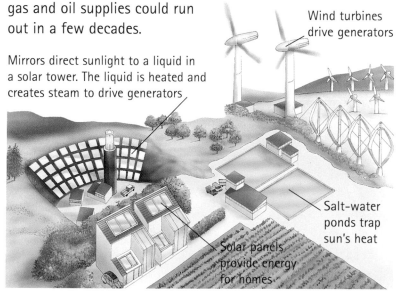

Mirrors direct sunlight to a liquid in a solar tower. The liquid is heated and creates steam to drive generators

Wind turbines drive generators

Salt-water ponds trap sun's heat

Solar panels provide energy for homes

What are fossil fuels?

Coal, oil, and natural gas are all fossil fuels. They are called this because they are made from the fossilized remains of plants and tiny animals. Oil is made from the remains of tiny sea creatures that lived millions of years ago. Oil rigs (above) are used to extract oil from deep beneath the sea bed. An oil rig is a platform with powerful drills that cut down into the rock. Once the oil has been reached, it is pumped up and sent down pipelines to land, where it is made into gasoline and other products.

How can we get energy from water?

Water is a very valuable source of energy. It can be used to produce electric and mechanical power. Hydroelectric plants use water from rivers, waterfalls, and dams to spin enormous wheels called turbines, which generate an electric current. Ocean waves are also a good source of power (right). Waves rock floats that absorb the energy and use it to drive pumps. The pumps force a liquid to spin the turbines and generate electricity.

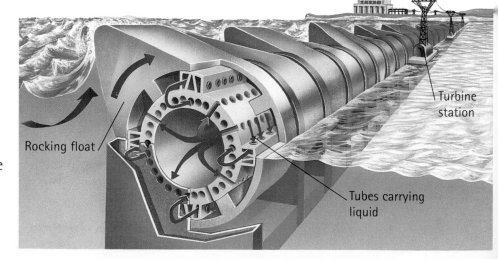

Rocking float

Turbine station

Tubes carrying liquid

What is nuclear energy?

Nuclear energy is created when tiny particles called neutrons are fired at uranium atoms, causing the atoms to split (below). This is called nuclear fission. It releases more neutrons and heat, which is used to generate an electric current. Fusion, which occurs on the sun's surface, also creates nuclear energy. This energy makes the sun shine.

Sun's surface

Neutrons released

Heat energy produced

Neutron fired at uranium atom

Atom splits

Uranium atom

Quarry

Surface ores removed with power shovels

Shafts and tunnels access ores deep below surface

How are metals extracted from the ground?

Metal deposits near the ground's surface are the easiest to extract. Miners scoop them out, using explosives to break up any layers of rock in the way. If the metal ores are deep underground, miners have to tunnel through solid rock and cut them out. Stones used for building, such as marble and slate, are cut or blasted from the ground in a process called quarrying.

Quick-fire Quiz

1. Which of these is a fossil fuel?
a) Coal
b) Wind
c) Sunlight

2. Which atoms are split to create nuclear energy?
a) Uranium
b) Cranium
c) Magnesium

3. Which of these is a renewable resource?
a) Coal
b) Wind
c) Oil

4. How much of the Netherlands is reclaimed land?
a) One eighth
b) One fourth
c) One half

Is it possible to create new land?

Since medieval times land has been reclaimed from the sea. In the 1920s a large part of the Netherlands (right) was made usable, or reclaimed, by enclosing it with a massive dam. Today roughly one fourth of the land area of the Netherlands is reclaimed land. Italy, Japan, and England also have areas of reclaimed land.

Land reclaimed
before 1900
after 1900

Netherlands

Do all countries have the resources they need?

Raw materials and energy sources are not evenly spread throughout the world. Russia, the United States, and Brazil are rich in minerals, but some countries must import raw materials. Heavy materials are transported by sea—oil is shipped in huge tankers (right).

Taking Care of Earth

Humans have done a great deal of damage to Earth. Forests have disappeared, natural vegetation has been cleared to make way for farmland and cities, and industrialization has polluted the oceans, rivers, and atmosphere. Governments and environmentalists have looked for ways to reduce the damage humans have caused.

What is recycling?

Many of Earth's natural raw materials have been used up by humans. Some materials, however, can be made into something new, or recycled. For example, old glass bottles and jars can be crushed and melted to make new glass objects. Aluminum cans, plastic bags and bottles, newspapers, cardboard boxes, and old clothes can also be recycled.

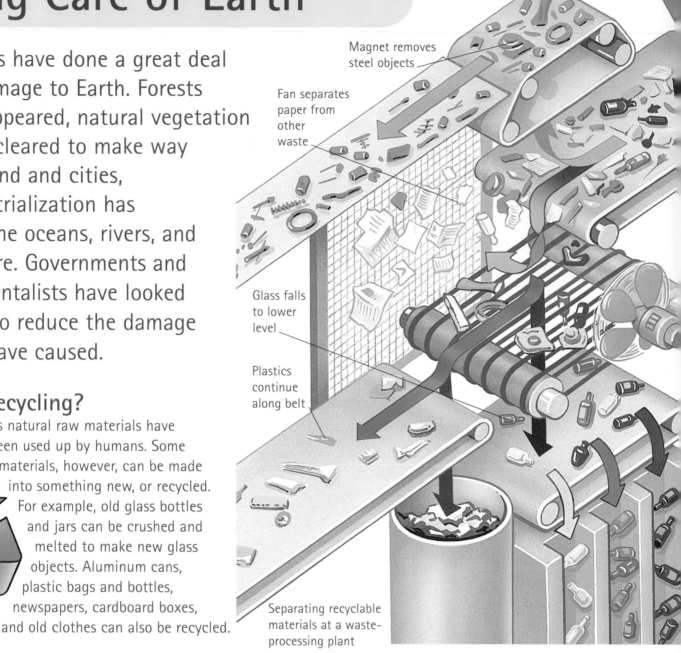

Mixed waste

Magnet removes steel objects

Fan separates paper from other waste

Glass falls to lower level

Plastics continue along belt

Separating recyclable materials at a waste-processing plant

Where is there a hole in the sky?

About 15 miles (25km) up in the atmosphere is a thin layer of ozone that protects Earth from the sun's ultraviolet rays. Certain chemicals, such as CFCs (chlorofluorocarbons), have destroyed part of the layer, creating a hole over Antarctica. CFCs were used in refrigerators, aerosols, and food packaging, but they are now banned.

What are wildlife reserves?

Hunting and the destruction of natural environments have caused many animal species to become endangered or even extinct. Wildlife reserves provide a protected, natural wilderness where endangered species can live without risk from game hunters.

How is industrial land reclaimed?

1 Factories release smoke and chemicals into the atmosphere, polluting land and rivers. Garbage dumps and mines destroy natural vegetation.

2 Garbage dumps and old industrial areas can be cleared and covered with a thick layer of soil to be used as recreational land. Open-pit mines can be flooded to make new lakes.

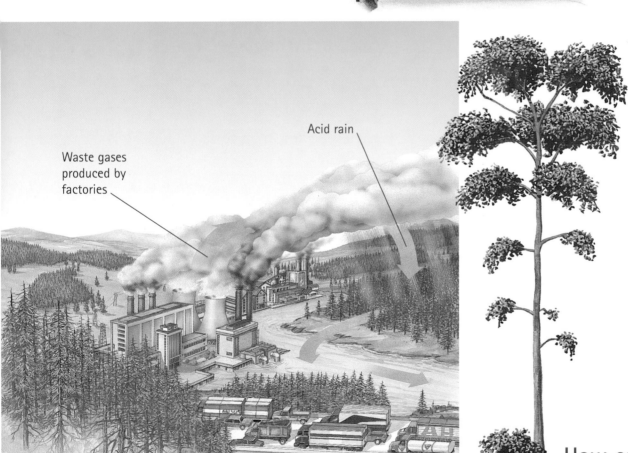

Acid rain

Waste gases produced by factories

What is acid rain?

Burning fossil fuels releases sulfur dioxide and nitrogen dioxide into the air, where they mix with water to form a weak acid. This eventually falls as acid rain (above). Acid rain can fall far away from the source of the pollution. It can kill many trees and acidify rivers and lakes, harming wildlife. Reducing our use of fossil fuels will help reduce the problem of acid rain.

How can we combat deforestation?

To prevent the destruction of rain forests, or deforestation, tropical timber is grown in plantations. Special fast-growing trees that can grow several yards each year are cultivated.

39

Index

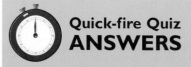

Quick-fire Quiz ANSWERS

Page 5 Earth's Formation
1. a   2. c   3. b   4. a

Page 7 Crust to Core
1. b   2. b   3. c   4. a

Page 9 Water
1. c   2. b   3. a   4. b

Page 11 Land
1. b   2. b   3. b   4. c

Page 13 Earthquakes
1. a   2. c   3. a   4. b

Page 15 Mountains
1. c   2. b   3. a   4. c

Page 17 Volcanoes
1. c   2. a   3. a   4. a

Page 19 Rocks, Fossils, and Minerals
1. a   2. a   3. c   4. b

Page 21 Climate
1. c   2. b   3. b   4. c

Page 23 Weather
1. b   2. b   3. a   4. a

Page 25 Polar Regions
1. b   2. a   3. a   4. c

Page 27 Deserts
1. c   2. b   3. a   4. a

Page 29 Grasslands
1. a   2. c   3. c   4. c

Page 31 Forests
1. c   2. a   3. a   4. b

Page 33 Life on Earth
1. b   2. a   3. c   4. a

Page 35 Human Landscape
1. c   2. b   3. c   4. a

Page 37 Earth's Resources
1. a   2. a   3. b   4. b

Page 39 Taking Care of Earth
1. c   2. b   3. c   4. b